accent on

SOLOS

LEVEL THREE

by
william gillock

ISBN 978-1-4234-7578-1

WILLIS MUSIC

EXCLUSIVELY DISTRIBUTED BY

HAL•LEONARD®

Visit Hal Leonard Online at
www.halleonard.com

World headquarters, contact:
Hal Leonard
7777 West Bluemound Road
Milwaukee, WI 53213
Email: info@halleonard.com

In Europe, contact:
Hal Leonard Europe Limited
42 Wigmore Street
Marylebone, London, W1U 2RN
Email: info@halleonardeurope.com

In Australia, contact:
Hal Leonard Australia Pty. Ltd.
4 Lentara Court
Cheltenham, Victoria, 3192 Australia
Email: info@halleonard.com.au

Contents

[Certain titles were updated in 2020.]

Drifting Clouds

William Gillock

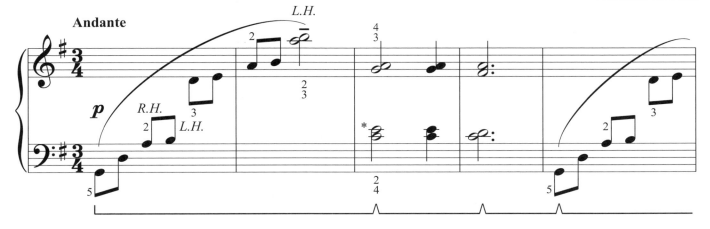

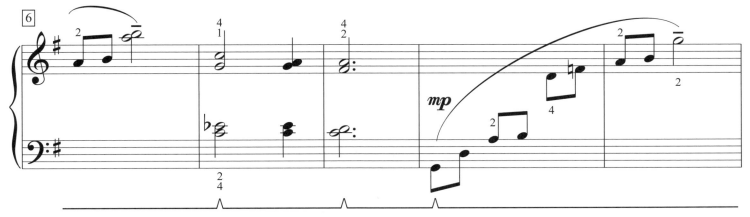

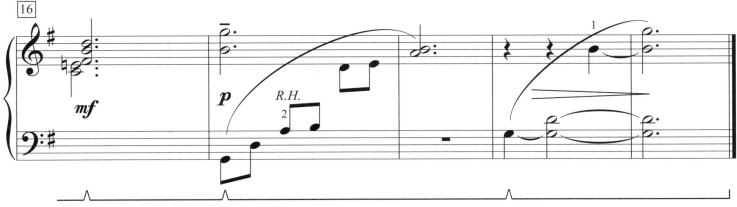

*Originally written as E-flat; Gillock revised in 1993.

Sliding in the Snow

William Gillock

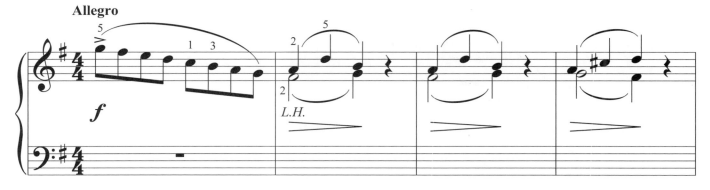

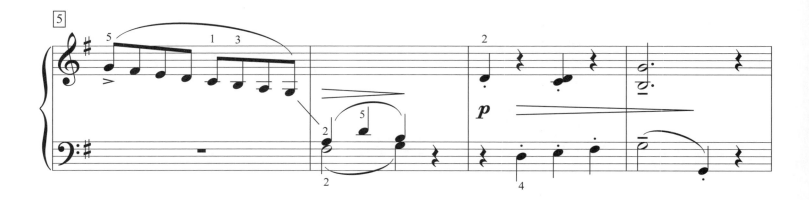

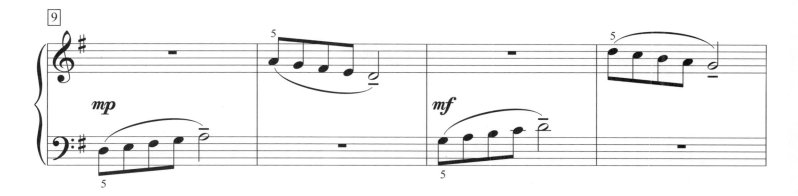

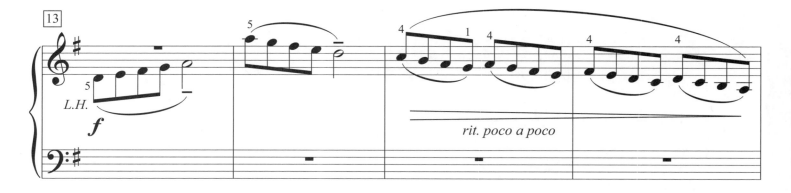

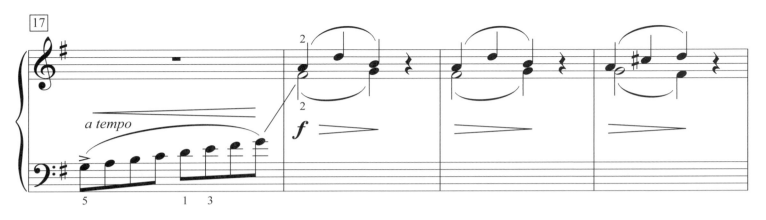

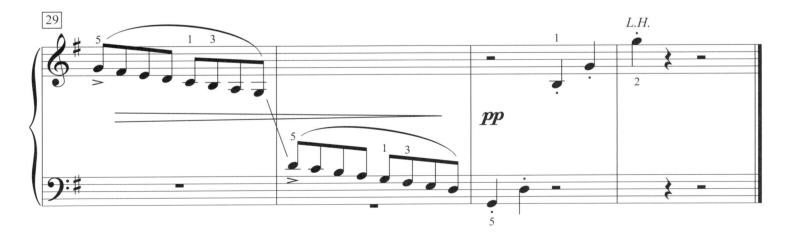

The Queen's Minuet

William Gillock

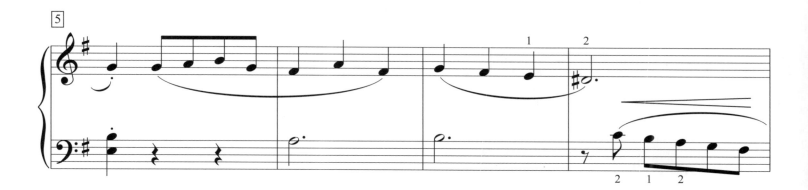

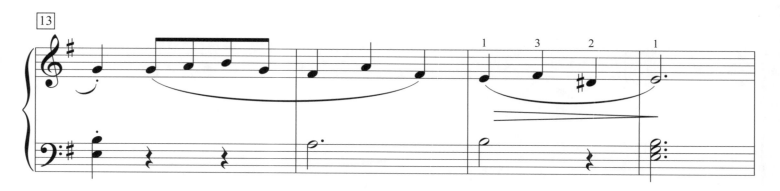

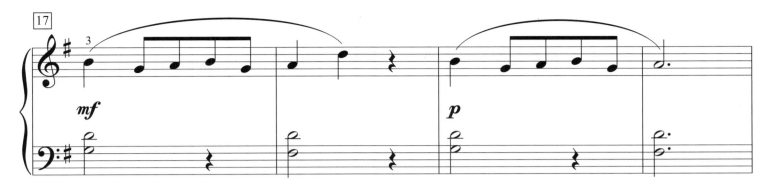

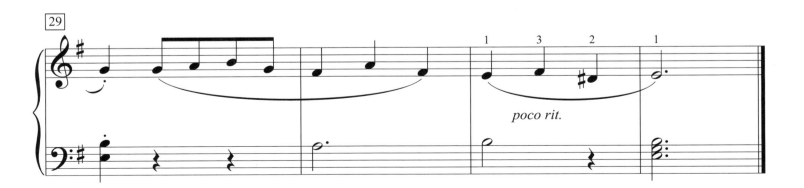

At the Circus

William Gillock

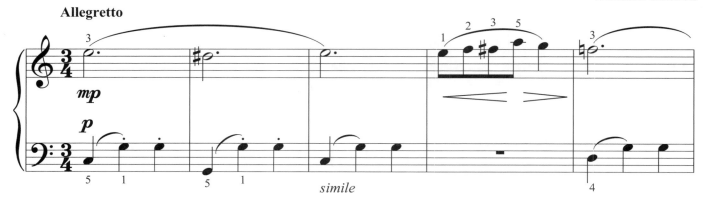

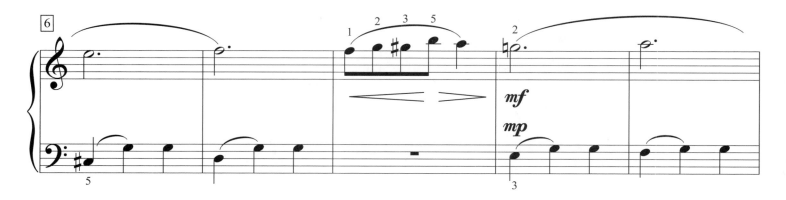

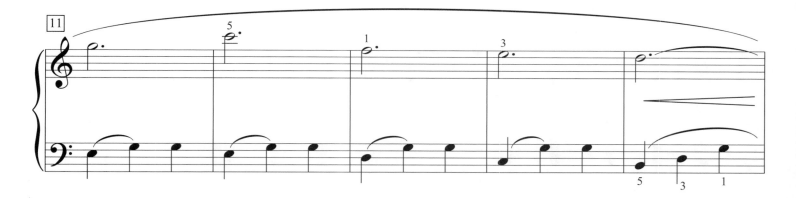

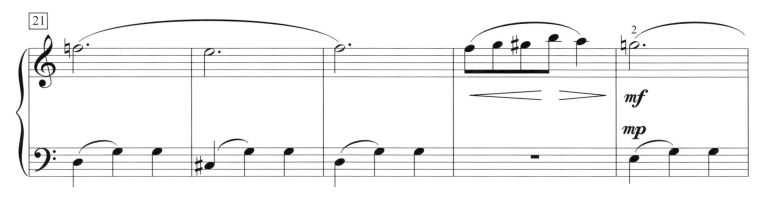

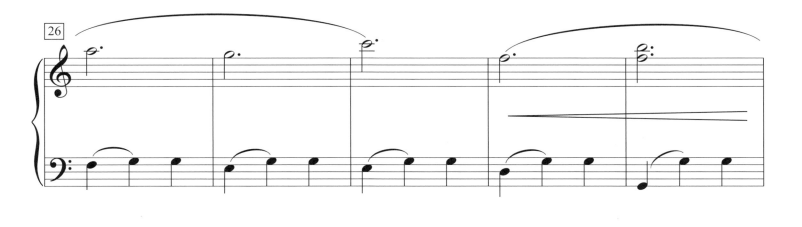

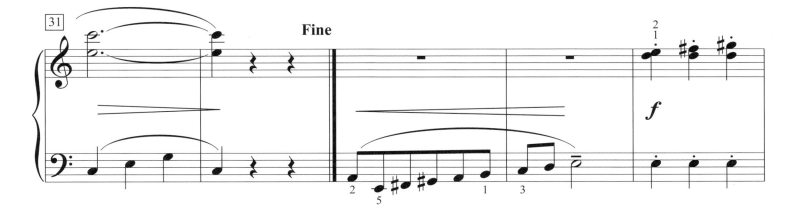

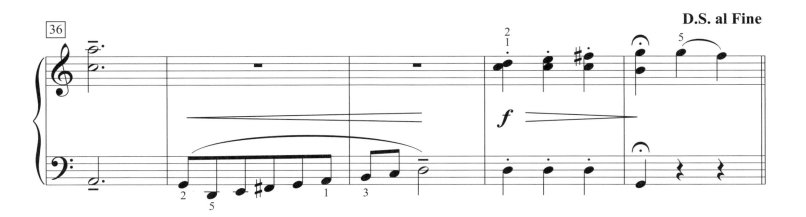

Swinging Beat

William Gillock

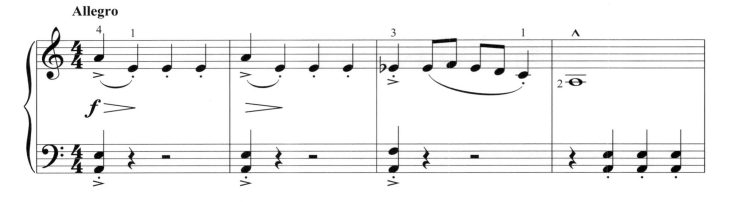

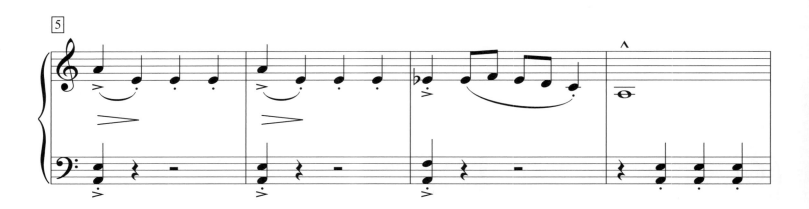

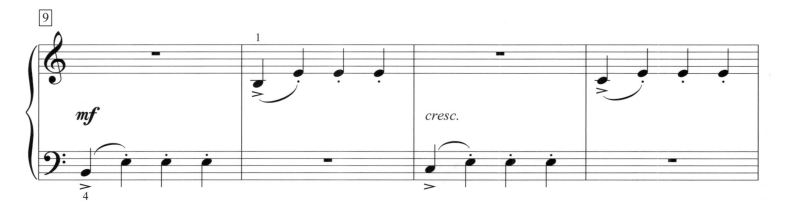

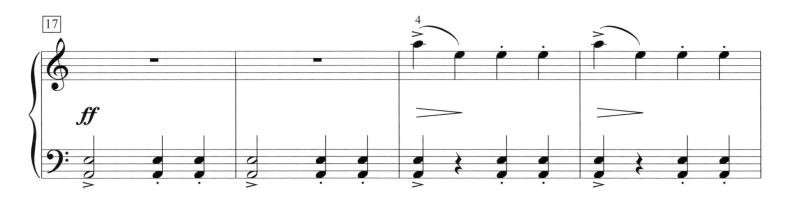

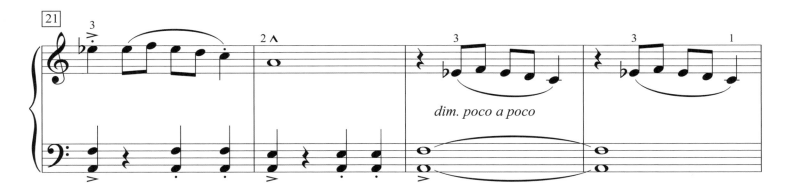

Dance of the Toys

William Gillock

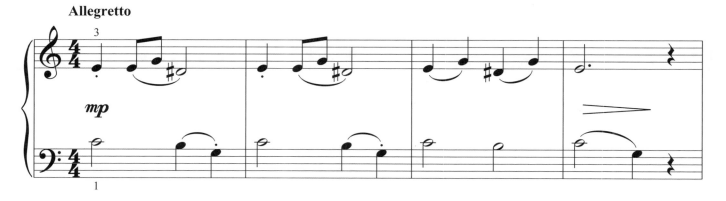

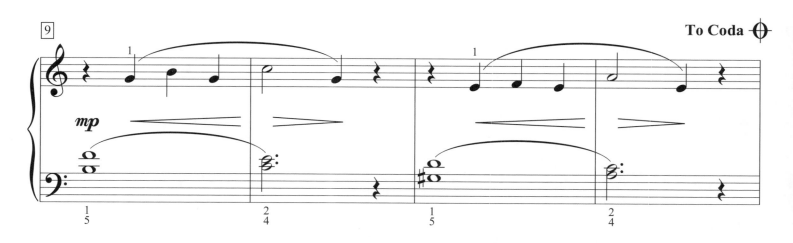

D.C. al Coda

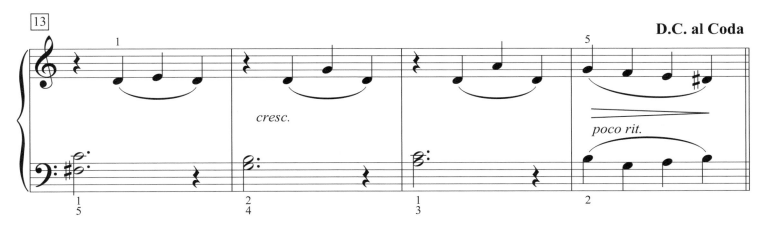

CODA

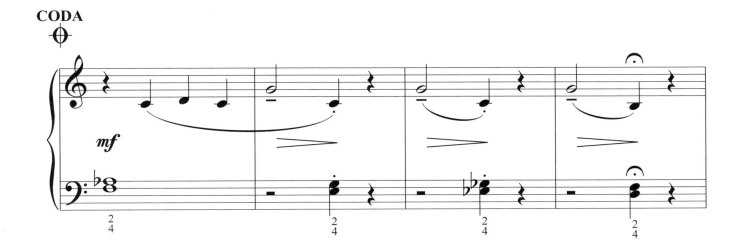

Enchanting Marketplace

William Gillock

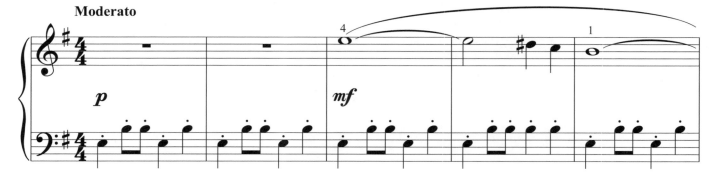

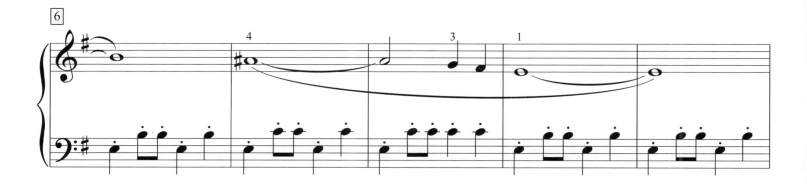

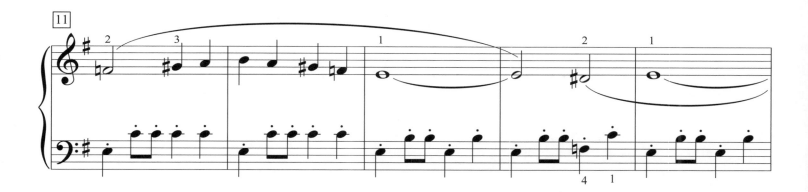

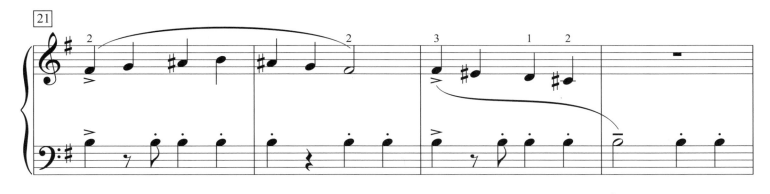

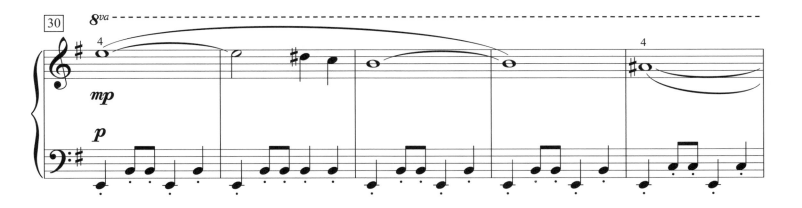

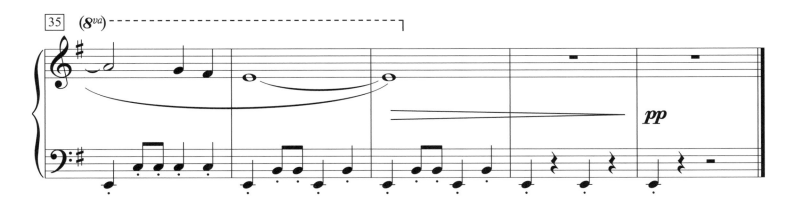

Summertime Blues

William Gillock

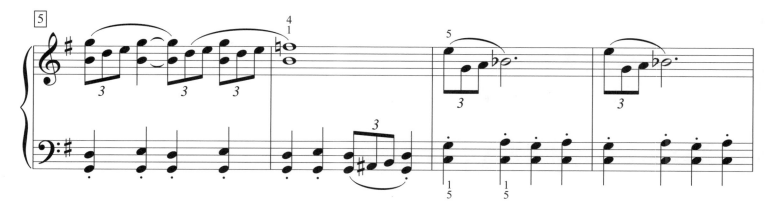

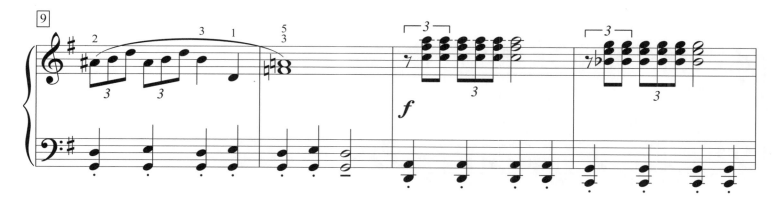